A Seven Bears Publishing production, 2019.

ISBN:
978-1-7344259-1-8 (epub)
978-1-7344259-0-1 (hardback)
978-1-6906384-1-4 (paperpack)

SEVEN BEARS
P U B L I S H I N G

Pithy Poems *for* Peculiar People

Priscilla Doremus

"But ye are a chosen generation, a royal priesthood, a holy nation, a peculiar people, that ye should show forth the praises of Him who hath called you out of darkness into His marvelous light."

— *1 Peter 2:9*

Other Books by Priscilla Doremus

So, You Call Yourself a Christian

Prayers for Times of Crisis

Focus: A Daily Devotional

Focused Daily on God's Best

Plea Bargain

Contents

Author's Note

The purpose of the poems on the following pages is to draw you into a closer walk with Jesus Christ. If they do not do that, then I consider this project vanity and a failure. Some of the poems may appear to be directed toward preachers and churches. Please know how much I dearly love and respect those who preach God's truth—my father and brother among them. I love, equally, God's established Church. It is the counterfeit gospel that I take aim at in these poems, and the wolf disguised as a shepherd of which I warn. They are many.

We are each so easily led astray. May we hold tightly, unswervingly to our Savior, Jesus Christ, and hold our brothers and sisters of faith by the hand that we might be protected from the deceiver, Satan.

May we allow nothing and no one to take first place above or crowd out our love for the Father, our Abba, the One True and Living God, Jesus Christ alone.

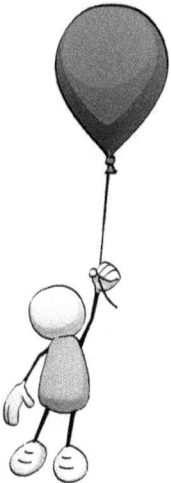

But Jesus said unto him,
"Follow me; and let the dead bury their dead."

—*Matthew 8:22 KJV*

—Priscilla Doremus
www.priscilladoremus.com

Peculiar

My neighbor is peculiar
He says he knows the Lord
I've never heard him swearing
His children are adored

He's always kind and giving
To everyone in need
He doesn't scream and shout out loud
Or tell each selfless deed

He doesn't coat with sugar
The truth he speaks just fine
He's not given to greed or glut
Or excesses with wine

He isn't like the neighbor
That lives just down the street
He says that he knows Jesus Christ
But isn't quite so sweet

He says his faith is private
And that one shouldn't judge
But when I needed him to help
This neighbor didn't budge

This neighbor's not peculiar
He's like that one church bunch
They act more like a country club
That gossips over lunch

I want to be peculiar
I want to know the Lord
But this gift that He's given me
I just cannot afford

My neighbor said that Jesus
He bought this gift for me
He lived and died and lives again
This grace—from Calv'ry's tree

It seems, oh so expensive
To little minds like mine
But then, He is the Son of God—
Once human and divine

Now I believe in Jesus
He's changed me, I am free
I once was lost, but now I'm found
Was blind but now I see.

The House That Words Built

There was a house that words built
A sullen, sorry place
No shutters on its windows
Deep darkness on its face

It had no light around it
No landscaping or trees
And, if you wanted inside
Nobody had the keys

This house had heard such hatred
Unhappiness and strife
It couldn't do one thing right
Despised—it had no life

The owner never cleaned it
Or tended it at all
It was in such disrepair
The walls were soon to fall

"You're ugly and I hate you"
Said Owner to his house
"I wish that you would crumble
You're useless, you're a louse"

This owner's words were heeded
The house crumbled and fell
Its crash so loud the echo
Still heard—the neighbors tell

The other house that words built
A grand, glorious place
With light filling each crevice
Its windows trimmed with lace

This house was filled with laughter
With dancing, and with joy
Oh, such a welcoming place
To every girl and boy

Its owner praised and bubbled
And gushed about the place
"I love it here! Such beauty!
Come join us in this space!"

And as the owner praised it
This house began to hum
It gleamed with glory and grace
And stands for years to come

So, as you're building your house
Be careful what you say
Each spoken word has power
And you'll live there one day.

Ode To The Preacher

A preacher's a fanciful soul
With tending the sheep as his goal
He shepherds the flock
In his curious frock
While toting his tea as he goes

Some say that he is a queer one
He never does anything fun
He dare not get winded
Much less be offended
Lest someone decide that he's done

Some wish he'd breathe fire and brimstone
Most folks like a gentler tone
Yet, all people agree
When he's on bended knee
They want their requests to be known

Some think his truth-telling is odd
A few smile and give him a nod
Though some have repented
The crowd's not been dented
Keep preaching, O Preacher of God.

Miss Davis

Miss Davis is seventy-three
She's come since a grasshopper's knee
She wears on her face
That she's earned that pew place
So, you better not mess with Miss D

Miss Davis's favorite seat
The one that is ever-so sweet
"Is five from the front"
She says with a grunt
It's cooler—she can't take the heat.

Sanctimonious Sanctuary

Our church is such a lovely place
Perfect flowers in each vase

Velvet cushions on the pews
Choir robes in different hues

Hymnals dusted, floors are swept
Stacks of Bibles neatly kept

Every nook and cranny cleaned
Polished, perfect and pristine

Communion wafers, wine to drink
Each cup topped off to the brink

Three big screens with words on them
Pictures, movies, every hymn

There is but one small thing amiss
Not one heart here looks like this.

Preacher's Wife

Expectations everywhere
Most aren't even needed

Pious folks all want to talk
Want their voices heeded

Preacher's wife, she tries to please
Each one's daft opinion

Not set in lagnappe and ease
No calling her minion

The Father sees her struggles
And all the tears she cries

He sees each ball she juggles
And every tear He dries

She gives her best to all y'all
With no thanks in return

So, be kind to this sweet doll
Lest all your ways she learn.

Forgive Me

Forgive me, Lord, for all my wrongs
Your will is where my heart belongs

Forgive me when my faith is weak
When of Your love I fail to speak

Forgive me for the harms I cause
The times I disobey Your laws

Forgive me when I'm like this earth
Chasing things of empty worth

Forgive me for the chances missed
Too many of them here to list

I lay these things now at Your feet
And kneeling at Your mercy seat

Your goodness draws me to repent
For by Your love Your Son You sent.

Sister Sally

Sister Sally seems a saint
When looking at a glance
Listen now, she really ain't—
In any circumstance

I've seen her when she's shopping
At our local grocery store
The bill was really whopping
And she went to buy some more

At Wednesday's potluck dinner
She only brought one dish
It could have been a winner
But it didn't go with fish

One time I caught her dancing
When nobody was around
Just some peculiar prancing
And she made a happy sound

And then there was that time
I saw her in a bathing suit
It was smaller than a dime
But her friends said it was cute

Last week I saw her car parked
Outside the liquor store
The bag she had was unmarked
Oh, she's rotten to the core

What's that you say, you like her
Much more than you like me
I guess I'm much more broken
Than Sister Sally be.

Pauly Wants A Preacher

Pauly wants a preacher
Squawks Mary's mockingbird
He mocks and talks each morning
Of the sermons he has heard

Give the preacher money
He'll send this video
The preacher says this each day
On his weekly morning show

Five, ten, fifteen, twenty
Each one gets different gifts
He promises a blessing
As your pocketbook he sifts

Pauly wants Miss Mary
To find a new broadcast
A preacher who knows God's love
Not a shyster who talks fast.

Mornings With Jesus

I rise to meet the brand-new day
Expectant
What will He say

His voice to me is whisper soft
Father
Won't speak aloft

And though I've felt His two-by-four
Enveloped
His love is more

He speaks to me and I will hear
Completely
I will not fear

He holds me closer than the earth
Within
He gives me worth

Embrace me with Your love divine
Jesus
You are all, mine.

Quibble Quibble

Quibble quibble, Mrs. Dibble
Gossips, gripes and argues much
She's tried to stop but just keeps on
About the music, mood and such

Squabble squabble, Mr. Wobble
Before, during, after church
Of such things as pews and parking
And he's done his own research

Quibble squabble, Dibble, Wobble
Is there pleasure in each moan
You ought find a brand new calling
Hush your mouth and chew your bone.

Tradition

Tradition is a nice word
I like it very much

I've heard it almost all my life
In schools and church and such

It doesn't mean to hurt you
Or cause you any pain

It simply wants its own way
It wants things nice and sane

Jesus said we shouldn't void
God's Word for our tradition

But many didn't like that
They accused Him of sedition

They didn't like things shaken
Or different from the norm

In fact, this non-tradition—
It started quite a storm

So, if you've always done things
The way you always know

Just blame it on tradition
But don't expect to grow.

Pity The Pastor

I pity the pastor
He hasn't a clue
Of all that the people
Would like him to do

I pity the pastor
He don't make a lick
And has to keep working
Whenever he's sick

I pity the pastor
He's trying to please
The good Lord, but people
Judge each little sneeze

I pity the pastor
He's got no fair chance
Of living life freely
Without a man's glance

I pity the pastor
You pity him, too
Perhaps it will free him
From me and from you.

God's Coloring Book

I like the way You color, Lord
The way You color me
The shades You use, the different hues
As bold as they can be

You never mind the lines, Lord
You color way outside
I like it, though, You let me know
I never have to hide

Sometimes You use a crayon
To color on my page
A marking pen, and now-and-then
A paintbrush takes the stage

The strokes are all so perfect
Each one glides on with ease
Some fat some thin, erasing sin
'Til everybody sees

I think it looks like You, Lord
I never knew You could
Not what I thought, what others taught
You color, oh so good.

Ode To The Preacher's Kid

Preacher's kids are challenged
By all the church expects
They live their life in such a way
As not to have regrets

They always obey Daddy
With halos shined and straight
And never miss a service
Or ever show up late

Preacher's kids are crazy
And some of them are wild
At least that's what they've told me
Since I was just a child

They like to get attention
Like any other kid
But not the way that Mom likes
(Don't tell her what I did)

Preacher's kids are special
And different as can be
They're also perfect angels
I know 'cause one is me.

Let Us Pray

Dear Father, may we always be
Soft enough to bend our knee

Unashamed to bear Your name
Reminded of the way You came

Full of love that overflows
With joy and peace and faith that grows

Let us always shine Your light
That guides us through the dark of night

Help us to repent of sin
That we may be restored again

And boldly come before Your throne
That by our lives You may be known.

Road Rage In The
Church Parking Lot

Deacon Dunham parks his car with front side facing out
He makes the whole world wait for him whilst he turns about

Miss Amy's in a hurry (it's because she's late again)
With every ounce of self-control, she doesn't honk at him

Then there's dear Miss Albom with her walker right in tow
You couldn't possibly get mad at this one going slow

The church has added speed bumps to protect its little ones
But, speedy elders whip 'round them like they were made for fun

We smile and wave at officers who lead us to our place
Yet, soon as they are out of view we make an angry face

"She nearly hit me!" Billy cries. "Church parking lots are rough!"
Good thing that God sees all we do and witnesses this stuff.

I Give Him Praise

My heart and soul extol the Lord
And praise His holy name
For all good things come from His hand
Our lives are not the same

As when we walked in darkness
We lived in bondage and in chains
To a yoke of slavery
To sin, until He came

He came and we adore Him
For He adored us first
He loves us and sings o'er us
My soul—no longer cursed

With all the joy and praise I know
I'm longing to impart
This tribute that I bring today
I bring with all my heart.

The Building Fund

Give, give, give
The people want to live
In a bigger, better building
With pillars, cornice, gilding
Long halls and big classes
Big windows and stained glasses
That everyone will tell
The Spirit here doth dwell
But have they yet forgotten
What His love hath taught them
His Spirit not contained
In building, tent, or frame
But in your heart and mine
His light in us to shine
For all the world to see
Oh, may we ever be
His building on this earth
To show others His worth
And may we give and give
To help the whole world live
Where never comes the night
Enveloped in His light.

The Do-Nothings

Mr. and Mrs. Do Nothing
Have come to church today
They sit in the very same pew
As they did the last Sunday

They put in the very same thing
When the gift plate is passed
And they say the very same thing
To the one who walks in last

They help with the very same work
When they need a volunteer
And serve in the very same way
It's why others hold them dear

I don't understand them
And can't reprimand them
Why all the to-do about nothing.

Conquering
The Congregation

There is a new preacher in our town
His name is Reverend Leroy Brown

He isn't from around these parts
So, doesn't know the old church farts

He starts out preaching soft and sweet
And gradually turns up the heat

Old farts don't like it—not one bit
George says, "It's time this preacher quit"

They plan and scheme to run him out
Not knowing what the Lord's about

But Preacher, he knows how to pray
Looks like this preacher's here to stay.

The Journey

I started on a journey that I didn't plan to take
While minding my own business on a road down by the lake

A man there saw me fishin'—I was struggling with my line
His face was kind and gentle, and his eyes saw clear through mine

He said, "I'd like to help you—I can show you a new way"
My friends, they all ignored him—my heart longed for him to stay

"Sir," I said, "Please tell me . . . what is this new way you know
I only know this one way—show me, please, before you go"

The man, he took my fishing line and cast it on the lake
His hands were sure and confident, the cast made not a wake

There was no hesitation as he reeled the line back in
The fish he caught was massive, I could see from just the fin

"Tell me, Sir, your secret, if you please, before you go
What makes your way so different—tell me, please, I've got to know"

"The Father is the difference—He sent His Son from up above
To show the world His mercy, to give each one His love"

"How can I have this difference, Sir, can it come down to me
I want the peace I see in you, I want this love I see"

"Receive His one and only Son, that's how to have real life
Repent of sin, believe in Him, abandon this world's strife"

I did what this man told me and was baptized at the lake
My life is filled with joy, for now a different path I take.

Busted In The Baptistry

Susie said to Preacher
Would you check the baptistry
The temperature must be just right
The child is three-plus-three

Preacher went to check it out
He put his big toe in
But when he slipped and fell
He just decided on a swim

He took off all his clothing
With an hour or so to spare
But then he thought it best
If he kept on his underwear

Miss Susie went to fetch him
Not counting on the sight
Preacher simply smiled and said
The temperature's just right.

Hypocrisy And The Hypocrite

The church is full of hypocrites
I hear one fella say
He tells me that's the reason
He won't come to church today

He tells me there's hypocrisy
In preachers that he hears
All they do is entertain
And tickle young men's ears

He doesn't give a flyin' flip
About the offering plate
The building fund, the work they've done
Or that he shouldn't hate

He doesn't like formality
Or following the rules
He said he'd had enough of that
When he was back in school

He said they're all a bunch of fakes
Don't practice what they preach
He says he's better off spending
The day down at the beach

But one day he'll be golfing
Or hunting in his blind
And when the good Lord calls his name
He'll wish he changed his mind.

Of Hymns And Hers

One group wants the hymnals
Another wants the screen
"The old words are more meaningful"
Says Mrs. Klopfenstein

"The new songs speak to my heart"
The young one echoes back
They are not meant to give you stress
Or cause a heart attack

The music man, he tries to please
Each group as best he can
He mixes up the old and new
In hopes they'll understand

This music, whether old or new,
We raise unto our King
And He inhabits each one
Of the praises that we bring.

On Eagle Wings

On eagle wings I ride the wind
My freedom He has bought

He conquered sin, death and the grave
'Twas for my life He fought

So, I could soar above the clouds
And reach new heights each day

With courage, strength, joy and resolve
I fly, come thou what may.

Thoughts About Thinking

I often have thoughts about thinking
The very best thinkity thoughts

But often my thoughts about thinking
They think a bit more than they ought

The thoughts swirl and swirl in my noggin
Not knowing which way they should go

Sometimes I am quick and I catch one
I snatch it from way on down low

I tell it it's not in the right place
It needs to think higher than this

Rise up from the low place to find Him
Think thinkity thoughts of His bliss

I tell it to dwell on the Father
The wonderful deeds He has done

Whose ways are far higher than my ways
With all of life's victories won

So, if there's a thought that you're thinking
And, it's just a thinkity thought

Just tell that old thought that you're thinking
With no means to go where it ought

"Thought, I'll take you captive to Jesus"
Obey Him and I know you'll see

The thinkity thoughts that you're thinkin'
Will end up where each one should be.

Sermon Song

Sing a song of sermons
A pulpit full of rhymes
Four and twenty sermons
For these troubled times

When the first was spoken
The Church began to faint
Wasn't it a grand gift—
A gift fit for a saint

The saint was in the office
Counting out the plate
The preacher kept on preachin'
'Til everyone was late

The sinner snuck out early
To beat the lunchtime zoo
But when he went to order
The meal was sermon stew.

Simon The Sinner

Simon the sinner
Was full of disgrace
The shame of his sin
He wore on his face

Then he repented
He turned from his sin
Simon met Jesus
Let living begin!

Songbird

I hear Him each morning
He calls unto me
With sweet voice He sings
From the top of His tree

He sings, "Come and join Me
Come be My delight
Come sing with Me, Sweet
One, I'll help you take flight"

"Come try out your wings on
The winds of this day
Together we'll soar
To new heights, come what may"

He calls in the evening
His song still as sweet
He bids my return
To His loving retreat

He shelters me under
His wings strong and sure
The sound of His voice
Still so soft and so pure

Sing over me, Songbird
I want for Your song
To lift me on high
You are where I belong.

Crystal Clear

I see things clear as crystal
The way things ought to be
The way that God intended
Before sin lived in me

Before I took my first breath
Before I turned from Him
And started on my own road
A road so dark and dim

I see things clear as crystal
Not how I used to see
For I have met the Savior
And now He lives in me

I used to see things cloudy
As in a mirror's glass
Not knowing how imperfect
How dim and overcast

How can I see things clearly—
So different than before?
I've gone to life eternal
To live forevermore.

A New Humpty Dumpty

Humpty Dumpty
Sat on a wall
Humpty Dumpty
Had a great fall

All of God's grace
His love and compassion
Put Humpty together
In glorious fashion.

A Better Bo Peep

Little Bo Peep
Has lost her sheep
And, can't tell where
To find them

She calls each by name
And bearing their shame
Rejoices that she
Has found them.

A Nimbler Jack

Jack be faithful
Cut the wick
Jack, stay away
From the candlestick

Jack kept praying
Jack said "no"
Jack was unscathed
From his head to his toe.

An Ode To The Tongue

The tongue is a fiery fellow
A woman at best that's a shrew
But taming this dangerous fellow
Is something no human can do

She says things on one hand that flatter
The other hand gossips and bites
She has no more rein on her nonsense
Than what raging fire she ignites

One piece of advice I shall give you
Keep captive each thought unto Him
Be prayerful and think before speaking
Don't open your mouth to each whim.

Denomination Dilemmas

There isn't a section for Baptists
Nor Catholics nor Lutherans, too
Don't look for a sign that says Coptic
Though, no doubt, there will be a few

No need for that t-shirt that tells them
The church house to which you belong
Your seat and your status won't matter
You won't have your own pew or throng

Oh, what will we do up in Heaven
No labels on me and on you
How wonderful it will be up there
We'll praise Him together, anew.

The Visitation Vignette

No one visits anymore
They'd rather send a text
They're just too busy these days
With all that they have next

No one wants to visit
The sick, the lame, the poor
They'd much rather be out shopping
For things that they adore

No one cares to visit
The widow or the blind
They say that they're not led there
Or that they're not inclined

To visit lonely people
Or those they do not know
But, Jesus bids us follow Him
Dear friend, you, too, must go.

Get Me From
The Church On Time

Hurry, Preacher
I can't wait
Finish up, or I'll be late

Got some tickets
They are hot
If I'm late, I will be shot

Meeting people
They won't wait
They just don't appreciate

All God's goodness
Or His love
Sent to us from up above

Wait a minute
Why am I
Rushing so to say goodbye

Lord, change my heart
Soften me
For the world Your love must see.

Of Prodigals
And The Perfect

Older brother, that is me
Nearly perfect, you can see

Baby brother, what a brat
Me, me, me is where he's at

Took Dad's money, ran around
Selfishness was so profound

Spent the money, came on back
Says he's on the narrow track

Dad is happy, I am not
'Cause the fatted calf he got.

The Tentative Tither

Tentative Tither, what is your deal
Seems on your wallet there is quite a seal

Tentative Tither, why don't you give
Are you afraid that on less you can't live

Tentative Tither, give up the ghost
Do you think hoarding will give you the most

Tentative Tither, read Malachi
Chapter three, verse ten, please give it a try.

Of Faith And The Faithless

Where's your faith, O faithless
How do you claim His name
You seem to want a perfect life
With someone else to blame

When things do not go your way
Or how you want them to
You simply claim to be confused
About what you should do

Time to grow, O faithless
Beyond your simple ways
To love yourself and others, too
And serve Him all your days.

Abandon

Lord, help me to abandon
The world and all its ways
To follow after Jesus
When no one else obeys

I want to take up my cross
And follow after You
Your way gives light to darkness
When Satan's way ain't true

Your angels come and help me
When I send You my prayers
You bend down close to listen
Even if no one cares

I thrill to serve You, Father
And follow where You lead
Because it's on the cross You died
And for me You did bleed

O, may we e'er abandon
The lure of other things
To serve the One True Living God
Who is the King of Kings.

Can I Get A Witness

Can I get a witness
For the Lord today
Someone to tell things He's done
To shine a Sonlit ray

Someone unashamed of Christ
Who died upon the tree
And rose again on that third day
To banish Calvary

Has He done some good for you
Please tell someone this hour
Think it through, open your eyes
Proclaim His holy power.

Of Sheep And Shepherds

Some sheepfolds and some shepherds
Are different from the rest

Some sheepfolds wander aimlessly
And can't keep up at best

Some shepherds don't know how to lead
Their motives are all wrong

They thought to get some easy pay
They're where they don't belong.

If I Had A Nickel

If I had a nickel
Every time I saw
Someone turn their back on God
Or someone break the law

If I had a nickel
Every time I heard
People use God's name in vain
Or say a dirty word

If I had a nickel
Every time I dodged
Someone on a cell phone
Or a complaint was lodged

Then, I would have some money
A whole great big ol' gob
I wouldn't have to work for things
And I could quit my job

But if I had a nickel
For the times that you
Bowed to pray at bedtime, or
Before the food you chew

And, if I had a nickel
When you helped the poor
Or gave to those most needy
As you were once before

Oh, if I had a nickel
When one turns from their sin
And leaves it all to follow
Along the road most thin

I just might have a nickel
For the offering plate
And, it would trounce the gob I got
With Jesus' interest rate.

Whitewashed

Let us not be whitewashed
All pretty on the front
But inside just a filthy mess
All cancer with no shunt

Let us not be whitewashed
Yet filled with dead men's bones
Incurring wrath and anger from
The One true love has shown

Let us be of pure white
Whom Christ has cleansed of sin
Sharing love and Good News
Again, again, again

Let us be of pure white
The kind that doesn't show
That crimson stain sin left behind
Now washed as white as snow.

The Backslider

The slip and slide has nothing on
Miss Greta from the choir
Takes one step forward, ten steps back
Her life's one few admire

She says she just can't help herself
That that's what grace is for
It's sad she doesn't understand
Her life's worth so much more.

Reverent Reverend

Our reverend is so reverent
With flawless, perfect hair, this gent
To all the perfect schools he went
Not even belly button lint
This man for this one church was meant
The staff thinks he is heaven sent
No flaws, not even one small hint
But if we find one, he'll repent
I think we'll keep him for a stint.

A Pithy Prayer

Thank you, Father
For Your love
Sent to us from up above

Please forgive us
For our sin
May we not do it again

Humble our hearts
Make them soft
Help our spirits dwell aloft

Urge us listen
To Your voice
Guide us as we make each choice

Teach us to love
Everyone
As we were taught by Your Son

Amen.

Sinner's Sonnet

Sing a song of sinners
But don't just sing of that
Tell of how we're saved by grace
We won't stay where we're at

Sing a song of sinners
The glories Christ has done
Tell about His miracles
The victories He's won

Sing a song of sinners
But move beyond the sin
To see the One True Living God
Who died yet lives again!

Praise Jesus

People praise the pastor
People praise the church
People even laud the lawn
And hymnals on their perch

Why not praise our Jesus
Why not give HIM laud
He's the One, He gave it all
Oh, precious Son of God.

Sitting Still

Lord, help me to sit still
And listen to Your voice
To know that when life's hard
You'll help me with the choice

Help me to be quiet
And patient as I wait
Knowing You have never been
And never will be late.

Attitude Of Gratitude

I'm thankful for this day, Dear Friend
And all that You've placed in it
I'm grateful for Your guiding hand
That keeps my pathway lit

I'm longing to obey You, Lord
To show gratitude to You
Though I could never pay You back
For making my life new

I want to pay You homage
Though that's not near enough
My life must be Your symphony
Even when times are tough

Oh, may we always thank You
In all we do and say
For how we live each day and hour
Will show the world Your way.

Of Struggling Sinners

The only time we struggle, friend
I'm talking about sin
Is when we let the demons reign
The demons from within

People try to complicate it
Make it seem so hard
But Jesus said be like a child
Just playing in your yard

He told us to obey the law
He's written on our heart
It's really very simple, too
No need to be real smart

So, if you are a confused soul
Still struggling with your sin
Surrender all to Jesus Christ
And let His Spirit win.

Of Sleeping Saints

The saints have all been sleeping
In the pews where they once sat

Forgetting how to serve and pray
They've gotten nice and fat

They never miss a fellowship
A potluck or a mealtime

But join you in the morning prayer—
You won't see them at kneel-time

You see, they're busy sleeping
So, don't bother them just yet

They haven't had their beauty rest
It's very hard to get

Now, once they've finished sleeping
And doing what they do

Ask them if they're ready now
To stop warming the pew.

It Won't Be Like
This In Heaven

It won't be like this in Heaven
Popularity won't reign

It won't be like this in Heaven
No, the folks won't be insane

It won't be like this in Heaven
Everyone will get along

It won't be like this in Heaven
"Praise His Name" will be our song

It won't be like this in Heaven
Condemnation is no more

It won't be like this in Heaven
We will hear the Lion roar

It won't be like this in Heaven
Everyone will bow the knee

It won't be like this in Heaven
Every tongue will confess Thee

It won't be like this in Heaven
Heaven help us, we'll be free.

The Pasture

The Father bids me come to Him
And lay in pastures green
Escaping from a world that's often
Cold and cruel and mean

He leads me by the waters still
Restores my very soul
His pleasures are forevermore
When earth here takes its toll

He feeds me at a table
When my enemies surround me
His goodness chases after me
Ne'er ceasing to astound me

He comforts me at death's dark door
And so, I do not fear it
For what could there e'er be to fear
When His love keeps my way lit

He oils my head and fills my cup
Goodness and mercy there, too
And in His big house, I will live
Forever I'll be brand new.

Before The World
Began Today

Before the world began today
The evening stars shone bright
And each one had a different tone
And hue to pierce the night

The melodies of God's own thought
Sang perfectly in tune
Adorning each dark corner piece
And dancing with the moon

Before the world began today
Life seemed but just a dream
While Jesus held me safe and sound
Embraced by love's fierce theme

The future doesn't scare me
No need for any plan
For Jesus holds and held me then
Before the world began.

Tell Somebody

Shout it from the mountaintops
Sing it from the sea
Tell someone your story
Of how Jesus set you free

Tell them how He changed you
Share with them His love
Tell them how God sent His Son
To earth from up above

Tell them He was perfect
Yet was crucified
Nailed upon a cruel cross
'Twas for our sins He died

Tell them on the third day
He rose triumphantly
Tell the world that Jesus lives
He lives to set them free!

Our Only Hope

Seems to be a missing link
'Tween what saints and sinners think

One has hope in Christ alone
By His blood they've been atoned

Other has no hope at all
Seems their vision's much too small

Lord, please open up their eyes
Help them, please, to recognize
Satan has a shrewd disguise

Worldly ways won't help them cope
Jesus is our only hope.

I Will Go

Yes, Dear Father, I will go
And tell the world You love them so

I will tell them that You came
To heal the sick and mend the lame

You gave the blind man back his sight
And raised the dead from dark to light

I will tell them how You cried
That it was for me You died

I will tell them so much more
Eternal life is what's in store
Life with You forevermore

I will go, Lord, take me there
I'll share Your Good News everywhere.

Why

Why are you so undisturbed
About the twisting of God's Word

Can't you see they're wolves—not sheep
Why are you so sound asleep

Serving Satan, he's their man
It's all in *his* master plan

Do you see it—most do not
Some just hope they won't get caught

These twisters serve another cause
They serve themselves, they chase applause

Worldly fame, all me, me, me
Repentance, Hell—they cannot see

Wake up, sinner, in the pot
They're boiling you, and you're quite hot!

Feel Good Gospel

Just went to church and I feel good
Learned things I'd not understood

Preacher never said repent
No sin—don't know where it went

People there were dressed so nice
Heard of virtue, heard no vice

Blessings and prosperity
Humanness, philosophy

All these things will come my way
Once I leave the church today

Don't forget to write that check
Lest your life become a wreck.

My Jesus

Jesus bled and died for me
Gave His life to set me free

From the chains of sin that bind
Sin that held me trapped and blind

Perfect, sinless life He gave
Sinful ones He came to save

Called me to repent of sin
Said I must be born again

Fully God and fully man
I believe the great I Am.

The War

Dear friend, we're in a war today
It's true—no matter what you say

That battle is for one lost soul
Condemning it is Satan's goal

A shred of truth wrapped in a lie
He told Eve she wouldn't die

He uses weak ones in his con
Wake up! The battle rages on!

Open My Eyes

Peel back my eyelids closed tighter than tight
Squinting in pain, so afraid of the light

Show me the beauty my soul longs to see
In spite of the dark things still warring with me

Help me to truly repent of all sin
And live in the light of His Spirit within.

My Defender

The liars and the haters
Whisper all around
Pretending all the while
That I can't hear a sound

But, if I listen closer
Quieting my heart
His words of truth defend me,
Deflecting every dart.

Bully Pulpit

There's a bully in the pulpit
Preacher's gone astray
From the truth that Jesus said
Would never go away

Not your normal bully
This preacher that we've got
He smiles and tells us funny jokes
And makes us laugh a lot

We feel good when we leave there
All warm and fuzzy, too
There's nothing in the whole wide world
We think we cannot do

But can't you see the lie here
The fallacy that's preached
He's taken out the Savior's truth
So no one will be reached.

Between Two Sinners

There He hung, between two sinners
Faultless lamb of God was He
Knowing that between two sinners
He died for you and died for me

One sinner mocked and scoffed at Him
Daring Jesus with no fear
The other said, "Remember me"
As his death lingered near

Jesus turned to answer Him
Before his life was through
This day you'll be in paradise.
Friend, which sinner are you?

Thermodynamics

The laws of thermodynamics
Are really quite simple, you see
They're all about heat and physics
And used to mean nothing to me

Now I see it's all about Jesus
Just like everything else He makes
This science makes heat more efficient
Helps us to understand earthquakes

Our Jesus is thermodynamic
Confused, my friend, why can't you see
The kindling made for your fire
He reclaimed on Calvary's tree.

Condoning Sin

I have the right to follow God
I have the right to not
But one way takes me to a place
That's very, very hot

Some people don't believe it
And make up their own lies
Not ever seeing Satan's mask
He wears a thin disguise

But have we yet forgotten
God's truth—it changes not
Repent, believe, and Him receive
He's all the truth you've got.

The Prayer Room Is Open

The prayer room is open
So come as you are
With all of your baggage
Each wound and each scar

The Father will listen
He won't turn away
He'll bend down to hear
Every word that you say

Bring Him your praises,
Your burdens and cares
You don't need to have
Fancy words in your prayers

Let your heart sing to Him
Cry from your soul
He's near to the broken
He makes each one whole

Bring Him your reverence
Give Him your love
Thank Him for Jesus
Sent down from above

The Father is waiting
Each day and each night
The source of all hope
Finds in you His delight

His miracles chase you
They long for a place
To show forth His love
Shedding mercy and grace

The prayer room is open
So come right on in
Hurry to hear Him
Have faith and begin.

Home Again

We long to see loved ones who've gone on before
Those bright, friendly faces we miss and adore

Each one placed indelible prints on our heart
We cherish them, carry them, like works of art

God fashions things perfectly through life and death
In every split second and to our last breath

So, with God as my Savior, I'm kissin' the pig
Then I'm home again, home again, jiggity-jig.

Poeem-A-Wep

In the jungle, the mighty jungle
Our Lion does not sleep
He hears each child's call to Him
He hears each precious weep

Come near our Lion of Judah
Bow down before His throne
Each one He longs to rescue
To guard you as His own

Our Father, Savior, Warrior
This jungle I'll not fear
For You have come to save me
I'll hush for You are near.

Pretty Lady

There is a pretty lady at the office where I work
Nobody even sees her—most are mean and one's a jerk

She does for everybody, waits on each one hand and foot
Without so much as thank you, Cinderella in her soot

But she just keeps on going, keeps on smiling come what may
It does not matter what they do, she cares not what they say

I think that she is beautiful, though others just can't see
Beyond all of the wrinkles, the white hair, oh, mercy me

I'm glad that Jesus sees and knows how beautiful she is
But you should stop and tell her, too, she is a child of His.

Sweet Answered Prayer

My Father bends to listen to me
When I bow to pray
Faithful, ever faithful listening
To each word I say

Not only does He listen to me
But His answer's sure
Testing every motive in me
Knowing if it's pure

His answer's always better, though I
Often fail to see
The depth of His unfailing love,
Unfailing love for me.

His Call

He calls me, "Come and follow"
He whispers in my ear
But, do I hear His sweet voice
Oh, do I sense Him near

Or, have His calls gone silent
Because I hear Him not
Chasing dreams and fantasies
Not doing as I ought

Is it greed that grips me
Prestige, pride, or the norm
Or, am I just a rebel—
Unrepentant and lukewarm

I will turn aside from those
Whose hearts refuse to see
This day I now surrender
I surrender all of me.

Never In A Million Years

Never in a million years
Would I have thought I'd see
The heinousness of infants killed
Oh, how it impacts me

Never in a million years
Would I have thought that prayer
Would be removed from all our schools
No one would ever dare

Never in a million years
Would I have thought that God
Would be considered obsolete
And people we would laud

Never in a million years
Would I have thought Sunday
Would no more be the Sabbath rest
But just a time for play

Never in a million years
Would I have thought that you
Would not be in your old home church
My friend, I'm in your pew.

Electricity

It's the power and presence of God
Living inside us—our own lightning rod

It's His Spirit—the essence of change
Moving among us—our lives to arrange

As He pleases—vibrant and alive
Your key on His kite string—revive!

The Truth, The Whole Truth, And Nothing But The Truth

I stand here before you
My heart for to tell
The truth and the whole truth
So you may be well

I've nothing but truth
From His Word for to share
And keeping it inside
I never could bear

The perfect One, Jesus,
Came down from on high
To show forth His love
On a cross He did die

He took all my sins
And He took your sins, too
The Perfect One, poured out
For me and for you

He rose on the third day
And gave us new life
Sweet vict'ry o'er death
And an end to this strife

Now, won't you repent
Of your sins and believe
His free gift is waiting
For you to receive.

My Candy Bar

My Jesus is a candy bar
He's Father, Spirit, Son
Like chocolate, nougat, caramel
The Godhead, three-in-one

Enrobed in luscious purity
Oh, taste and see He's good
One taste, there's no resisting Him
As if you ever should

He's simply irresistible
There's nothing I want more
No person, place, or anything
Above Him I adore

Don't laugh or mock my Candy Bar
Perhaps you've never met
'Cause if you have, you understand
This craving that I get

My Jesus is a candy bar
Together we will dine
I'm hungry for Him every day
Oh, I'm so glad He's mine.

Much Is Required

To whom much is given
Of them much is required

To share with the world
Those things God hath desired

Not keeping for themselves
The things they've been gifted

But reaching a hand down
For one to be lifted.

A Walk

I took a walk outside today
Not for any grand reason
But wanting just to clear my head
Enjoying, too, the season

It started like most other walks
The breeze was nice and cool
I heard some children laugh and scream
While playing in their pool

The blue jays danced on up ahead
While chasing squirrels nearby them
I wanted so to join in, too
And, acted on my whim

I wasn't very graceful—no
The squirrels and birds stared at me
But didn't seem to mind so much
They let me join their party

I kept on walking after that
Not with a plan or purpose
But knowing that my Abba, He
Controls this world's strange circus

And He will guide each step I take
I need not fear the wild
For there is no one He loves more
Than me, His precious child.

Another Walk

I took another walk today
Escaping from my ease
And as I walked I heard my cares
Cavorting through the trees

This walk was in the morning time
Just me, myself, and I
And Jesus came—not quite the same
As other walks of mine

He whispered gently to me
Now that we were alone
He told me things I hadn't thought
Some things I should have known

His love—it overwhelmed me
I finally understood
The vastness of His plan for me
Our God is, oh, so good.

The Admonition

Who will admonish the teacher
When teacher's too busy to hear

And who will admonish the teacher
When student's too humble, too dear

Yes, who will admonish the teacher
She's gotten too lofty, I fear

Who will remind her to seek Him
To call with heart humbled and clear

She's gotten a wee bit too famous
I've not seen her heart shed a tear

Dear teacher, the throngs, they are calling
Calling, "Teacher, to Jesus draw near."

Before I Was A Kid

Before I was a kid
My Father knew my every thought
Before I was a kid
He sent His Son, my sins He bought

Before I was a kid
God saw me in my mother's womb
Before I was a kid
In Heaven He prepared my room

Before I was a kid
I was a sinner just like you
Before I was a kid
Sweet Jesus knew what I would do

Before I was a kid
My Jesus had a place on high
Before I was a kid
He called to me and bid me nigh

O, let me be a kid
With eyes that see just who He is
Joyful, loving kid
Content in knowing I am His.

Subject

The subject of this poem is of
Whom this one is subject to.

There really is no need for me
To subject you to what I do

Though all my doing since I've become
Subject to the King of Kings

Remains as subject—now and always
Only to the best of things

And what is this, "the best of things"
My life is subject to, you ask

It, simply stated, follows His truth
As His subject, that's my task.

Wake Up

Wake up, Sleeping City
Wake up, Sleeping Town
You've missed a few things lately
Since you've been laying down

The world, it's been a'changin'
Since you've been asleep
Your voice has not been heard much
Whilst you slept so deep

Wake up, Sleeping City
Wake up, Sleeping Church
Wickedness has taken hold—
Knocked you from your perch

And yet, your snores continue
Your dreams are, oh, so sweet
Evil dances round your bed
Tickling your feet

But, you don't even notice
You can't even tell
While you steal some beauty sleep
Your family goes to hell.

Humble Pie

My momma gave me humble pie
This evening for dessert
She told me that I needed it
I am a cocky squirt

I ate it rather slowly
Something started to occur
The thoughts of me and mine, mine, mine
Began to be a blur

Across from me, a sister
I now noticed in the room
A brother, dog, dad, mother
Oh my, how it all did bloom

So smart, so talented they are
To think I never saw
How yummy, too, this pie
That was delivered by my ma

Inside my heart a miracle took place
From that first bite
Such gratitude and joy
It's like I finally saw the light

So, if you're acting snotty
And Mom gives you humble pie
Enjoy each bite, it just might change your life
Don't ask me why.

Family Mission Statement

The purpose of this family
Is really very clear
To show the world how much we love
The ones we hold so dear

And, why is it we do this
Why do we love each one
It's all because He loved us first
He gave us each His Son

And, how is it we show them
That Jesus' love is real
We practice showing love at home
In each word, deed, and meal

So, let's show through our families
That Jesus is the way
Let's light the path to Heaven's door
So, they get there one day.

Mirror, Mirror

Mirror, mirror on the wall
I can't see myself at all

How does my reflection look
Just one glance at me You took

Do You dread to look at me
Am I hideous to see

How does my reflection seem
Perfect—no, that's just a dream

Must You turn and hide Your face
Drenched in sin I am—disgrace

Tell me, Mirror, what You see
Help me to be truly free

I, the Mirror, know you well
Much about you I could tell

I will tell you what I see
Listen to these words from Me

You have asked Me how you look
Just one look is all it took

You, My bride, are lovely, fine
I have called you, you are Mine

You have asked Me how you seem
Perfect—I am Elohim

Drenched in sin I see you not
Every stain from you I blot

Call to Me, repent and know
Beauty no one else can show.

Weary Traveler

Weary trav'ler, come and find rest
Take your place among the blessed

Lay down your great load
From this long dusty road

Let Him wash your feet
While you find sweet retreat

Come and drink from the well
Of His greatness you'll tell

Welcome home, weary trav'ler guest.

Surprise Me

Surprise me, Lord
You know I love
Surprises sent down
From above

Surprise me through
The things You do
That all the world may
Love You, too

Surprise me with
The thoughts You think
Way up high
Not rinky-dink

Surprise me in
Each unwrapped gift
And though I peek
You are not miffed

You surprise me
Every day
Surprising One,
With You I'll stay.

Twinkle, Twinkle

Twinkle, twinkle,
Morning Star
How I love
The way You are

Up above and
Down below
You will guide
The path I go

Twinkle, twinkle
Oh, Great Light
Keep me on
Your path of right.

Yabba Dabba Abba

Abba Father, I adore
Who You are, please show me more

Of the depth, width, height of You
Who takes all and makes it new

How You touch each tender strand
Of my life and make it grand

Wasting not one ounce or crumb
Feeding, beckoning to come

Leading me through every choice
I will listen to Your voice

With You I long to entwine
Abba, yabba dabba, mine.

Here Comes The Bride

I saw the holy city
Heaven coming down
Straight out of the sky above
Dressed in royal gown

Then I heard the shout out
From the throne on high
God has joined His people now
And no one else must die

God, Himself, doth dwell there—
Will wipe each tear away
No more sorrow, death or pain
His light will be the day

The Spirit and the bride say,
"Come, drink His living water"
No one e'er will love you more
Oh, precious son and daughter.

Investments

I looked at my investments
And took stock of each one
All stocks, savings, checking account
Each property and fund

Some were doing wonderfully
And some were doing good
Most were doing what I'd hoped
Performing like they should

Then Jesus gently whispered
Is this all that you see
Have you only earthly wealth
No investment in Me

Have you spent your life chasing
These things and wanting more
Or, is it Me you want, my dear
Just Me that you adore

When all is said and done here
And your life on earth is through
Where will your investments be
In Jesus or in you?

Posthumous Power

The power that we think we have
Is really quite misleading

When fame, fortune, position call
It's Satan's schemes they're feeding

But, if your life's a quiet one
And Jesus' way you're heeding

There is no doubt, once dead and gone
Your light will still be leading.

Oh, Come

You've heard the gospel message
You've heard it from your youth
You've run away with evil
The darkness veils His truth

But, it's not too late for you
Though night is closing in
When no man can turn aside
Please, repent of your sin

Good deeds will not save you
Or wash away your sin
Only Jesus' precious blood
His life living within

Oh, hear His voice, He's calling
Shouting, begging you to come
Don't wait another moment
Just turn around and run

His arms, they're held wide open
His embrace, none compares
Please turn to Him, dear sinner
His love is waiting there

And, with one final whisper
He calls, oh, come to Me
Before you take your last breath
Let Real Life set you free.

It Is Finished

It is finished
It is done
Your salvation
Has been won

By the shed blood
Jesus gave
Your soul and your
Life to save

So receive Him
Trust His way
Turn to Him and
Live, obey

He won't fail you
Never will
Every longing
He'll fulfill

Loved us first and
Loves us now
Never worry
Wonder how

Once in prison
Now, I'm free
Jesus, finish
You in me.

Author Biography

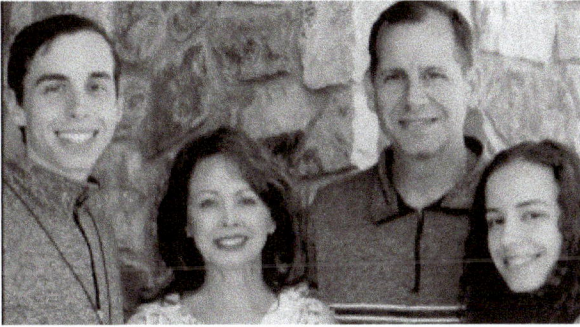

PRISCILLA DOREMUS is the daughter of a Baptist Minister who has enjoyed writing from the time she was big enough to hold a pencil. At age ten, she published *The Mysterious Mansion* in *Highlights* with the assistance of her uncle, Alan Cliburn, an established author.

She holds a Bachelor of Business Administration from Baylor University and a Master's in Educational Administration from the University of Houston—Victoria. She has worked for numerous years in the field of Insurance and Risk Management. Priscilla considers herself a homebody though she has traveled all over the world. She also enjoys baking and has become known around town for her chocolate chip cookies.

Diagnosed with a brain tumor in 2001, something Priscilla sees as one of the most wonderful blessings she ever received, she decided to get serious about writing. *Prayers for Times of Crisis* was her first nonfiction work.

Priscilla is a married mother of two grown children. She and her family currently live in Sugar Land, Texas, together with the family dog, Little Bear.

www.ingramcontent.com/pod-product-compliance
Lightning Source LLC
Chambersburg PA
CBHW051848090426
42811CB00034B/2251/J